STEP-UP Books

are written especially for children who have outgrown beginning readers. In this exciting series:

• the words are harder (but not too hard)
• there's more text (but it's still in big print)
• there are plenty of illustrations (but the books aren't picture books)
• the subject matter has been carefully chosen to appeal to young readers who want to find out about the world around them. They'll love these informative and lively books.

WHITE HOUSE CHILDREN

Imagine
• having soldiers camped in your house
• playing tag on the White House lawn
• having a pillow fight with the President of the United States
• meeting kings and queens

These are some of the experiences of children who have lived in the White House. The special lives of George Washington's grandchildren, Abraham Lincoln's sons, Teddy Roosevelt's six children, Caroline and John Kennedy, Jr., and Amy Carter are all here in this intriguing book.

WHITE HOUSE

by Miriam Anne Bourne

Step-Up Books   Random House

New York

CHILDREN

illustrated by Gloria Kamen

J
920
B

For the Lewis Family

The author and publisher wish to thank the following people for help in preparation of this book: Amy Carter; John Castellani, Assistant Director, Mount Vernon; Faith Collins, Deputy Press Secretary to Rosalynn Carter; Mary Hoyt, Press Secretary to Rosalynn Carter; Jacqueline Onassis; Geoffrey Ward, Editor, *American Heritage* magazine.

Copyright © 1979 by Random House, Inc. All rights reserved under International and Pan-American Copyright Conventions. Published in the United States by Random House, Inc., New York, and simultaneously in Canada by Random House of Canada Limited, Toronto.

Library of Congress Cataloging in Publication Data

Bourne, Miriam Anne. White house children. (Step-up books) SUMMARY: Describes the lives of the children and grandchildren of Presidents Washington, Lincoln, Theodore Roosevelt, Kennedy, and Carter. 1. Presidents—United States—Children—Biography—Juvenile Literature. 2. Washington, D.C. White House—Juvenile Literature. [1. Presidents—Children. 2. Washington, D.C. White House] I. Kamen, Gloria. II. Title. E176.45.B68 973'.0992 [B] [920] 79–529 ISBN 0–394–84094–1 ISBN 0–394–94094–6 lib. bdg.

Manufactured in the United States of America   1 2 3 4 5 6 7 8 9 0

Contents

Living in the President's House

What if your father or grandmother or uncle became President? Would you like to leave home for Washington, D.C.? Would you like to move into the White House?

That is what Presidents' families have been doing since 1800. Before that there was no White House. There was not even a Washington, D.C.

George Washington was our first President. At that time, the capital of the United States was in New York City. So George Washington and his family lived in New York City. A year and a half later the capital moved to Philadelphia. So the Washington family moved to Philadelphia.

Our second President was John Adams. He lived in the White House in Washington, D.C. The house was still being built. Many rooms were empty. The front stairs were not up yet.

Finally the White House was finished. It became a very special place. But do children like living in the President's house? Are there good places to play? Is life fun and exciting? Or do the children wish they could go back home?

George Washington's Nelly and Wash
(1789–1797)

Nelly Custis ran to a window.
"Grandmama," she cried. "Look at all the people on the street!" She ran to another window.

"Grandpapa! Look at the fire engine going by."

Grandpapa was George Washington, the first President of the United States. Nelly and her brother lived with their grandparents. The family had just moved to New York City.

Nelly was excited by life in a big city. She was used to Mount Vernon, a Virginia farm.

"Nelly is a little wild creature," her grandmother said.

Nelly's brother was confused by city life.

"Little Washington is lost in a maze," his grandmother said.

Nelly's brother had a long name. It was
George Washington Parke Custis.
Sometimes the family called him "Wash."
He was eight when Grandpapa became
President. Nelly was ten.

The American people wondered about
their first President. How would he act?
Like a king? They did not want a king.
But they wanted the President to be looked
up to by kings.

So the Washingtons had a fine coach.
It was pulled by six cream-colored horses.
The stable master put wax on the horses'
coats. Then he rubbed them to make them
shine. He kept the horses' teeth clean too.

Every Tuesday Grandpapa had a party
for gentlemen. Every Friday Grandmama
had a party for gentlemen and ladies.
Children were not invited.

Once Wash hid behind a curtain and watched. Nobody knew he was at the party but Nelly. Wash saw the feathers in a lady's hair catch fire. He saw a gentleman put out the fire with his bare hands.

There was a lot for Wash and Nelly to do in New York City. They went ice-skating. They went to see a tightrope walker. They went to the theater and the circus and a wax museum. They gave plays of their own with friends.

Wash went to a school with other boys. After school he and his friends played with balls and marbles. They beat on Wash's drum and fired his toy cannon.

Nelly went to a school for girls. She studied reading, spelling, writing, and arithmetic. She studied geography, French, and sewing. At home Nelly took painting and drawing lessons. She took lessons on the piano too. Nelly's grandmother made her practice a lot.

"Nelly played and cried and cried and played," said her brother.

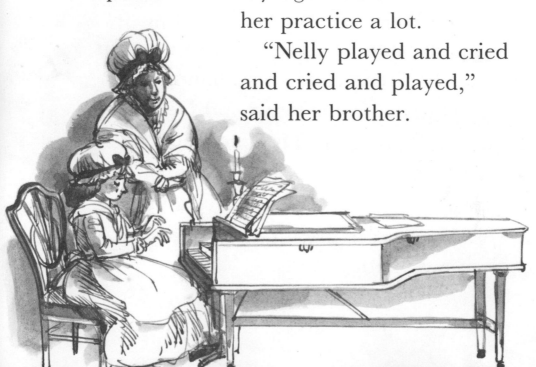

Nelly and her friends giggled a lot. They giggled when Nelly taught her dog tricks. They giggled when Nelly taught her parrot funny words.

Nelly's friends were shy with President Washington. They were a little afraid of him. Nelly was not.

Grandpapa often laughed at Nelly's funny tricks. Nelly laughed when "Dearest Grandpapa" told her tall tales. He said he saw a toad eat a firefly. The toad "lit up like a lantern," Grandpapa said.

Grandpapa did not joke very often. He was too busy running the country. A lot of people helped him. The secretary of state, the secretary of the treasury, the secretary of war, and the attorney general helped him the most. They were the first Cabinet.

President Washington listened to his Cabinet's advice. He thought for a long time before making up his mind. Some people said he was too slow and careful.

There was a lot to be careful about. The new government was in trouble. It had little money. Some whiskey makers in Pennsylvania would not pay their taxes. President Washington sent soldiers there to help collect the taxes. This new government was not to be sneezed at!

There was trouble in Europe too. France and England were at war. Each country wanted America's help. President Washington made a treaty with England. He thought the treaty would keep America out of the war. Some people did not like the treaty. They stood outside the President's house and shouted.

Inside Nelly and Wash did their homework. They tried not to be afraid of the angry crowd. Grandpapa looked sad and worried. He was lost in thought. Grandmama had a hard time getting his attention. She tugged on one of his coat buttons. Then Grandpapa looked at Grandmama and smiled. Nelly and Wash felt a lot better.

George Washington was in office two terms. By the end of those eight years he was tired and growing old. He wanted to move back to Mount Vernon. So did the whole family. President Washington refused to run for a third term. Vice-President John Adams was elected President.

The Washingtons packed 97 boxes and 14 trunks for the trip home.

"Do not forget the parrot!" Nelly reminded her grandfather.

"Grandpapa! Do not forget the dog."

"I would not mind much if we forgot them both," Grandpapa teased Nelly. But he did not forget them. Both dog and parrot rode home to Mount Vernon.

There were 14 Presidents between George Washington and Abraham Lincoln. Most of their children were grown up. But nephews, nieces, and grandchildren came to live at the White House.

Susanna Adams was the first child to live in the White House. She was the granddaughter of President John Adams (1797–1801). The new White House was cold and damp. Poor Susanna got sick with the whooping cough.

Mary Fairlie Tyler was the granddaughter of President John Tyler (1841–1845). She had a costume party at the White House on her third birthday. Mary dressed up as a fairy princess.

Abraham Lincoln's Sons (1861–1865)

Tad Lincoln stood on the White House roof. He curled both hands in front of one eye like a spyglass.

"It's an enemy ship," he told his brother Willie.

Willie put gunpowder into the toy cannon. He pretended to light a match. (The powder was really sugar from the pantry.)

"Ready, aim, fire!" Tad yelled.

"Ka-boom!" shouted Willie.

"We got the Rebs that time," said Tad.

Back and forth across the roof marched their friends Bud and Holly Taft. "We are tired of being on watch," they told the Lincoln boys.

"But you have to watch," said Willie. "It's your job."

"Soldiers who do not do their duty get shot," Tad said. He picked up the soldier doll that lay on the roof. "You see Jack? Jack fell asleep on watch. He will have to be shot."

The boys carried the doll to the garden. They began digging a hole for Jack's grave. The gardener saw them and spoke up. "Why don't you ask for a pardon?"

"Good idea," Tad said. He rushed into the White House. He pushed past a crowd of people. They were waiting to see his father, the President. Outside Papa's office was a guard.

"You may not go in," the guard said. "The President is meeting with his Cabinet." The men in the Cabinet were important. They helped Papa do his work.

"This is important," Tad said. He knocked on the door. Three sharp raps. Two thumps. That was his and Papa's "code."

"Come in," said President Lincoln. He smiled when he saw Tad. "What can I do for you, son?"

"Sir," Tad told him, "Soldier Jack is going to be shot as a traitor. That is unfair. He is not a traitor. I would like you to give him a pardon."

Papa opened a drawer. He took out a fresh piece of paper and wrote on it.

"If Jack is not a traitor, he should not be shot," Papa said. "Here is a pardon for Jack from the President."

Tad took the pardon and saluted his father. "Thank you, sir."

As Tad left, he heard Papa say, "He is a dear rascal."

The Lincoln boys played war. But a real war was tearing their country apart. Americans from the North and Americans from the South were killing each other.

People in the South were angry with Congress. Congress had passed laws they did not like. They were angry with the North for saying they should not own slaves. Southerners said they needed slaves to help them grow cotton. Selling that cotton was how they earned their living.

Eleven Southern states left the United States of America. They said the South was a new country. President Lincoln said the states could not leave the Union. Fighting started in Charleston, South Carolina, on April 12, 1861.

Soldiers fought terrible battles just across the river from Washington, D.C. People were

scared. Would Southern rebels attack
Washington…and the White House? Forts
were built around the city. Soldiers camped
in the East Room of the White House.

In spite of the war, Willie and Tad did
not always play war games. They gave
shows in their little theater. They rode
ponies. They popped corn. Sometimes their
long-legged father played leapfrog with
them.

Tad and Willie's big brother, Robert, was away at school. But Willie and Tad went to school in the White House. Their mother had desks and a blackboard put in the State Dining Room. A tutor tried to teach the boys. Willie learned fast. He liked to read and to write poems. Tad did not like to sit still at his desk.

"Let him run," his father said. "He will have time enough to learn his letters and get poky."

Tad was full of mischief. He found where the bell cords to call the servants came together. He pulled them all at once, and every servant came running.

Once Tad and Willie tied two of their
pet goats to a kitchen chair. They led the
goats into a parlor. Mrs. Lincoln was
giving a tea party there. She and the other
ladies were VERY surprised.

Tad broke a mirror in the front hall with
his new ball.

"Pa won't mind," he said.

"That mirror does not belong to Pa,"
Willie told him. "It belongs to
the United States Government."

Tad did not care. But he was afraid of bad luck. So he shook salt over his left shoulder. He tried to say the Lord's Prayer backward.

Bad luck did come to the Lincoln family. Of course, it was not because Tad broke the mirror. Willie got sick and died. His family was very sad. Mama could not stop crying. She cried about Willie. She also cried because people said mean things about her. They said she spent too much money on dresses and the White House. They said she was for the South.

It was true that Mama's brothers were rebels. Three of them had died in the war. Poor Mama felt awful that her brothers had been killed. But she wanted the South back in the Union. It made Papa angry when people called her a traitor.

After Willie died, the President and Tad
spent a lot of time together. They went to
the theater. They played with Tad's toys.
Papa liked to take the toys apart to see
how they worked. Then he put
them back together again.

Papa took Tad with him on visits to
army camps. Tad helped cheer up the
soldiers. He knew how to cheer up his
father too. Tad would run into Papa's
office, hug him hard, and run out again.
"This colt!" Papa called him.

It seemed as if the war would never end. Then President Lincoln did something he hoped would stop the fighting. He signed the Emancipation (ih-man-suh-PAY-shun) Proclamation (prock-luh-MAY-shun). That was a paper which said that all slaves in rebel states were free. The Proclamation made the South even more angry than before. But Lincoln knew he was right to sign it.

In 1865 the fighting did finally end. The Union was saved. America would be one country again.

But another terrible thing happened to the loving Lincoln family. A few days after the South surrendered, President Lincoln was shot and killed.

There were eight Presidents between Abraham Lincoln and Teddy Roosevelt.

Jesse Grant was a son of President Ulysses Grant (1869–1877). Jesse and his friends had a baseball club. They called it "K.F.R." Its whole name was a secret. President Grant thought that "K.F.R." must stand for "Kick, Fight, and Run."

"His Whiskers" was a White House goat. He pulled the grandchildren of President Benjamin Harrison (1889–1893) in a red cart. Once the goat ran down the driveway to the street. President Harrison was fat. But he ran after that cart lickety-split!

Teddy Roosevelt's Children (1901–1909)

Quentin was 3…Archie was 7…Ethel was 10…Kermit was 12…Ted was 14… and Alice was 17—when their father, Theodore Roosevelt, became President. What a crowd at the White House!

The Roosevelt animals moved in too. There were three dogs. Jack was Kermit's terrier. Skip was a black mongrel, Sailor Boy a retriever (rih-TREE-vur). Tom Quartz and Slippers were cats.

Even the guinea (GIN-ee) pigs had names. So did the turtles, hens, and rabbits. Bill was a horned toad. Eli was a parrot. What a zoo at the White House!

During one of his father's meetings, Quentin took four snakes from his pocket. He dropped them on a table and scared some senators silly.

When Archie had the measles, Quentin wanted to cheer him up. So he went to the stable. He got Archie's pony, Algonquin. Quentin led the pony into the White House and onto the elevator. He pushed the button for the second floor. Down the hall trotted Algonquin—right into Archie's room. Archie cheered up in a hurry!

President Roosevelt liked to play as much as his children did. He gave them rides on his back. He wrestled and boxed with the boys. He joined in pillow fights and games of tickley and fight the bear. Mrs. Roosevelt said she had five boys, not four. The President was her biggest "boy."

Teddy Roosevelt was the youngest President America had ever had. He was full of energy. He asked Congress to pass law after law. Some laws stopped giant companies from putting little companies out of business. He wanted some American land saved for people to enjoy, not to build on. So Congress voted for national parks.

Teddy Roosevelt sent 16 new battleships around the world. This "Great White Fleet" showed that America's navy was strong. "Speak softly and carry a big stick," said President Roosevelt. America's strong navy was "a big stick." It scared other countries away.

The President was always busy with something. But during family story time he sat still. He read *Alice in Wonderland* and *Peter Rabbit* out loud. He read folk tales, fairy tales, and stories from the Bible. He told ghost stories. He told Indian tales and lion stories.

As the children grew older, they went away to school. Archie and Quentin were

the only ones left at home. They found plenty to do. They roller-skated and bicycled. They played hide-and-seek. They slid down the White House stairs on trays.

They walked on stilts on the lawn and in the East Room. They raced in the hallways. Before an important dinner, they tiptoed into the dining room. They helped themselves to the candy and nuts at each place.

One day Archie and Quentin stuck spitballs on the paintings of the Presidents. Their father scolded them for that. Another day Quentin walked in a flower bed with his stilts. His father scolded him for that too.

When Archie went away to school,
Quentin was left alone. But he had a gang
of friends. Once Quentin and his gang were
riding in a trolley car. The President rode by
in his carriage. Quentin and his friends
thumbed their noses and wiggled their ears.
The President made a funny face right back
at them. The other people on the trolley car
were surprised. They had never seen a
President stick out his tongue and cross his
eyes.

Sometimes Quentin and his father took friends on walks. They walked five miles in a straight line. No one was allowed to walk around anything. Everyone had to keep going straight ahead, no matter what.

One day the new French Ambassador was invited for a walk. He wore a top hat and lavender gloves. He thought the President was going for a stroll. But a stroll was too dull for Teddy Roosevelt and Quentin!

They led the Ambassador and Quentin's friends into the woods. They jumped over fallen logs. They pushed through prickly bushes. They bent down under low-hanging branches. Bugs and spiders bit them. Cobwebs brushed their faces. None of that slowed them down. "Straight ahead," cried the President.

The French Ambassador's gloves became dirty. His top hat got cobwebs all over it.

A stream did not stop the Roosevelts either. They jumped from rock to rock. They walked across a narrow log. They waded through shallow water.

The French Ambassador's gloves got wet.
So did his fancy shoes. His top hat fell off
when he crossed the log. It floated
downstream. Quentin grabbed it.

On the other side of the creek were steep
cliffs.

"Carry on!" cried the President. His big
body hurried up the cliffs. Quentin climbed
up behind him. So did Quentin's friends.

The French Ambassador looked as if he
might cry. But he didn't. He put his hat on
top of his head and ran up the cliffs. He
passed Quentin's friends. He passed Quentin.

He got to the top just behind the President.

"Huzzah!" shouted Teddy Roosevelt. "Three cheers for the French! France has beaten Quentee-Quee."

Quentin grinned and pulled up his stockings. He looked a mess. But didn't he always! His tie was usually untied. His clothes were torn. His stockings refused to stay up. Quentin didn't mind. He liked to have fun, not worry about clothes.

The whole Roosevelt family had fun in Washington for seven and a half years. In 1909 a new President moved into the White House.

"I do not believe anyone has ever enjoyed it as we have," said President Roosevelt.

Quentin agreed. He told his father, "There is a little hole in my stomach when I think of leaving."

There were eight Presidents between Teddy Roosevelt and Jack Kennedy.

Charlie Taft belonged to Quentin Roosevelt's gang. He was the younger son of President William H. Taft (1909–1913). When Charlie lived in the White House, he liked to work the telephone switchboard.

David, Barbara Anne, Mary Jean, and Susan were the grandchildren of President Dwight Eisenhower (1953–1961). They drove battery cars in the White House driveway.

Caroline and John Kennedy (1961–1963)

A snowman greeted Caroline and John Kennedy, Jr., when they moved into the White House. The gardener had made it to welcome them home.

Caroline was three years old. John was two months old. Caroline helped their nurse take care of John. She fed him water. She patted him and talked to him. She tucked in his covers when he went to sleep.

Americans wanted to hear all about President John Kennedy's new baby. The newspapers told his weight, his length, and how many teeth he had. They told when he crawled and when he stood.

When John could walk, he liked to go to his father's office. He would hide under the desk. It had a secret door he could close. "Is the bunny rabbit inside?" his father would ask. And John would pop out. "It's John-John!" the President would say.

Another place John liked to play was the kitchen. He opened the cupboards and played with the pots and pans.

Whenever a helicopter landed at the White House, John got excited. He cried when the "chopper" took off. He wanted a ride. Sometimes he and his father played helicopter. John-John was always the pilot.

Americans were interested in Caroline too. They liked to hear about the cute things she did and said. Once Caroline saw her father on television and kissed the screen. "Silly Daddy," she said. One day

Caroline walked into her father's press conference. She was wearing a pair of her mother's high-heeled shoes.

The TV and newspaper people snapped
pictures as fast as they could. The President
was laughing. He thought Caroline was cute
too. He called her "Buttons" because of her
tiny button nose.

On the White House lawn were swings and a sandbox and a trampoline. Caroline and her friends could climb a ladder to a tree house. They could slide back down to the ground. There was also a large playhouse on the lawn. Once John fell against its step. One of his teeth fell out.

The playground was outside President Kennedy's office. Sometimes he opened the door and clapped his hands. The children came running in.

Caroline loved horses. She had a brown toy horse and cart she could pedal. She

had a toy stable with horses. Caroline's mother put her on a pony when she was 18 months old. When she was 5 years old, Caroline rode her pony Macaroni in a rally. They won a blue ribbon. When John was put on a pony, he said, "I want to get off."

Americans were interested in Mrs. Kennedy too. Women copied her clothes and hair styles. Jackie Kennedy made the White House a place Americans were proud of. She greeted many visitors from other countries. Mrs. Kennedy spoke French to French people. She spoke Spanish to Spaniards and Italian to Italians. She asked musicians to play and dancers to dance in the East Room. She filled the White House with beautiful furniture and paintings.

People were interested in the President's brothers and sisters and their children. Caroline and John had 18 Kennedy cousins! Everyone went to Cape Cod, Massachusetts, in the summer. The cousins played on the sand and in the water. They had family cookouts. They had pony cart, golf cart, and boat rides.

People were even interested in the Kennedy animals. Caroline's grandfather gave her a Welsh terrier named Charley. Mrs. Kennedy's dog was Wolfie, a big Irish wolfhound. Clipper was the

Charley

Wolfie

Tom

President's German police dog. Tom Kitten was a gray cat with yellow eyes. A canary, 3 parakeets, 13 ducks, and 100 goldfish lived at the White House. Debbie and Billie were hamsters. Sometimes they got loose.

Of course, people were interested in President John Kennedy. The new, young President wanted to make the world a better place to live in. He asked Americans to help him. And they did. They took a new interest in their country and the world.

The President started projects to help poor people in other countries. He asked Congress to pass civil rights laws. He wanted black Americans to have the same rights as white ones. He asked Congress to begin a space program. Everyone was excited eight years later when two men landed on the moon.

President Kennedy wanted to keep peace in the world. The United States and Russia were not on friendly terms. So Kennedy asked Russia and other countries to sign a treaty with America. Each country agreed to test no bombs. None in the air. None in space. None underwater.

The leader of Russia tried to be friendly with Caroline. He gave her a fluffy white puppy named Pushinka. Its mother once flew in a space capsule.

Important people from other countries often came to the White House. John learned to bow, and Caroline learned to curtsy. Sometimes John got his bow mixed up with a curtsy. Once Caroline curtsied so deeply to a king, she nearly fell over.

Mrs. Kennedy and some friends started a school at the White House. Caroline went to the school. One day Caroline's teachers took the children out on the roof to play. The children heard an officer shouting orders to some soldiers. They ran to the rail and looked over. On the lawn President Kennedy was welcoming the president of Algeria (al-JEER-ee-uh).

"Attention!" called the officer. "Attention!" cried the children. "Present arms!" called the officer. "Present arms!" cried the children. "Bang-bang," boomed the guns. "Bang-bang," boomed the children—21 times. It was a 21-gun salute. President Kennedy tried not to smile. He was afraid the President of Algeria would be insulted.

Every morning Caroline and John ran into their father's bedroom. While he ate his breakfast, they watched cartoons on TV. When an exercise program came on, the children did exercises. They tumbled all over the floor. Then they walked their father to his office.

Americans loved a picture of Caroline and John dancing in that office. Another

favorite was of "John-John" running to
welcome his father home.

The saddest picture was of the little boy
saluting the President's coffin. President
Kennedy was shot and killed (just as
Lincoln was). He was buried on John's third
birthday.

There were three Presidents between
Jack Kennedy and Jimmy Carter. All of
their children were teen-agers or grown-ups.

A daughter of President Nixon
(1969–1974) married a grandson of
President Eisenhower (1953–1961). Julie
Nixon and David Eisenhower met when
they were children.

Patrick Lyndon Nugent visited his
grandfather, Lyndon B. Johnson (1963–1969),
at the White House. President Johnson
was from Texas. So Lyn wore a Texas
cowboy suit.

Amy Carter (1977-   )

Wherever Amy Carter goes, Secret Service people go with her. They watch Amy and keep her safe. They even take her to school each day. Does Amy mind? Not a bit. She is used to having guards around her.

Amy's father, Jimmy Carter, was Governor of Georgia before he became President. People were interested in his family then, as they are now. Amy has always had reporters asking her questions. She has always had policemen around. She has always had guards.

Once Amy was at a pet show. She was busy enjoying the animals. She did not see what an elephant was doing. It was breaking the rope that held it. The elephant got loose. It headed right for Amy! Her Secret Service guards rushed to help her out of the way. One man picked Amy up. He lifted her over a fence. Now she would be all right, he thought. But the elephant crashed through the fence! Another guard lifted Amy back to the other side. This time she was safe.

"It was kind of scary," Amy said later. She was glad those Secret Service men were there.

The Secret Service protects Jimmy Carter too. As President, his life is special. But he tries to be like other Americans.

On his first day in office, Jimmy Carter walked to the White House. Presidents usually take that trip in a big car. But not Jimmy Carter! His family walked with him. Some of the way, Amy skipped. She was eight years old then. People clapped and waved. They felt that the Carters were a lot like them.

The Carters ARE like other American families in many ways. And Amy's life is not so different from yours. Amy goes to public school. On her first day there, she wore blue jeans. She carried a Snoopy bookbag. Amy goes on field trips and writes reports.

"There's a lot of homework," she says.

Like many children, Amy takes music lessons. She is learning to play the violin. Her mother takes violin lessons too. They practice together after breakfast. Sometimes while they play, Amy's baby nephew sings. The cat, Misty-Melarky Ying-Yang Carter, meows. Together they make quite a racket!

"Misty acts like she owns the whole White House," Amy says. "Grits runs and jumps over everything." Grits is Amy's puppy. Her new teacher gave him to Amy when Amy moved to Washington.

Amy became an aunt when she was eight years old. She has fun with her nephews and niece. She teaches them new words. The babies laugh when Amy stands on her head.

Amy also plays with her grown-up brothers and their wives. They play Ping-Pong and chess. They bowl in the White House bowling alley. They swim in the White House pool. They see movies in the White House theater. Not everyone can do those things at home.

Amy's life is special in other ways too. She travels around the world with her father. She goes to important White House dinners.

Sometimes Amy carries a book in case she gets bored.

"I like to read anything," she says.

Amy meets special visitors at the White House. One was Mickey Mouse. He came there from Disneyland for his 50th birthday. Amy shook his hand. Once a group of actors gave a play in the East Room. It was called "The Littlest Clown." At the end the actors lifted Amy onto the stage. They dressed her in a clown costume. They made her up with a clown face. She became "the littlest clown."

In that same East Room the Roosevelt boys walked on stilts. In fact wherever Amy goes in the White House, other Presidents' children went too. Amy watches TV in the Carter family room. That room was the attic where the Lincoln boys gave shows. It was Caroline Kennedy's school room. Amy rides in the White House elevator. Quentin Roosevelt led Archie's pony into that same elevator.

Amy has a tree house on the White House lawn. So did Caroline Kennedy. Amy plays freeze tag and throws Frisbees on the lawn. She tries to find secret places among the trees and bushes.

One day Amy and a friend found the Children's Garden. It was tucked out of sight.

"There was a wishing well," Amy said. "It

had pennies in the bottom." She giggled. "I shouldn't tell. We took the pennies out. Well, not all of them. Because it's three feet deep. And you get wet. Those pennies must have been there for years."

Who knows which White House children dropped them in?

ABOUT THE AUTHOR

Miriam Anne Bourne lives near Washington, D.C., with her husband and their old dog, Chippy. Their children have grown up.

Besides WHITE HOUSE CHILDREN, Mrs. Bourne has had 11 other books published. One of them is RACCOONS ARE FOR LOVING, a Random House book. Mrs. Bourne also owns and runs The Children's Book Shop, a mail-order bookstore for children. On the top floor of her house, Mrs. Bourne has a small office surrounded by trees. She calls it "the crow's nest."

ABOUT THE ILLUSTRATOR

Gloria Kamen has illustrated many children's stories and books. One of them, a book about Mount Vernon, was written by Miriam Anne Bourne. Ms. Kamen has also worked on an award-winning children's TV series. And she has done on-the-spot courtroom sketches for WTTG News, Washington, D.C.

Ms. Kamen had her art training at Pratt Institute and The Art Students' League in New York City. She later moved to Bethesda, Maryland, where she now lives with her husband, a scientist. They have three grown daughters.

DATE DUE	
DEC 1 2 1993	
OCT 1 4 1994	
JAN 27 1996	
SEP 8 1998	
FEB 1 1999	
JUN 1 2 1999	
JAN 1 9 2001	
MAR 0 9 2003	